"ASCENSION CODES"

When you can't fake it, how to become it!

Manisha Kohli

First Published by

ISBN: 978-93-5741-749-5

Price:

BLUEROSE PUBLISHERS

www.bluerosepublishers.com

info@bluerosepublishers.com

"Your thoughts shape your reality, choose them wisely. You are the sum total of the internal queries you hold"

- Manisha

A GUIDE TO TRANSFORMING LIMITING BELIEFS AND SHIFTING TOWARDS AN ABUNDANT MINDSET, TAKING CONTROL OF THOUGHTS, BELIEFS, AND EMOTIONS TO CREATE THE LIFE DESIRED.

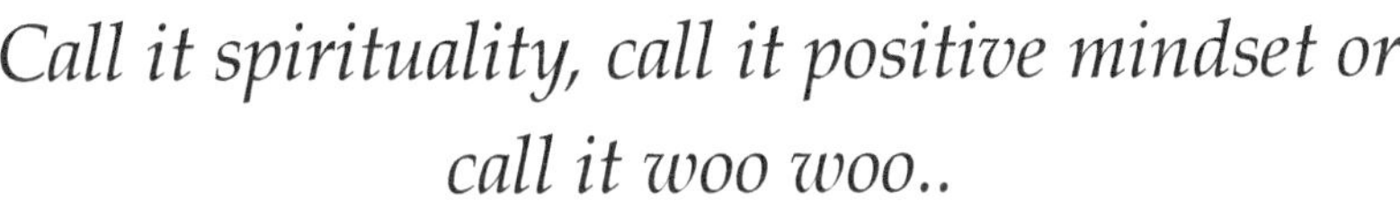

Call it spirituality, call it positive mindset or call it woo woo..

It's the stuff that works!

Contents

Introduction

We all crave transformation and the promise of something better. That subtle, yet undeniable longing for progress; a desire to level up in love, relationships, body or finances - it's real. The path isn't always easy as discovering that one thing which will set our world spinning with change can be daunting at times but just imagine how transformed you could feel if you managed to breakthrough from your present situation!

We essentially want to feel better. I am not talking about happiness, which perhaps remains the most unidentified end goal. I believe we are all striving to get one step better than where we are at right now. The quest for finding that one thing that'll change the status quo. The breaking point where we believe we need to level up. Possibly to define that something is the hardest part. That one change, it could be in love and relationships, in our bodies or in our finances. There is always that one thing which keeps wanting to shift and change so we will feel transformed.

Here is where the journey starts, to define that something. To identify the end goal in whichever area of life we feel lacking. I am no different, I wanted that something too, I wanted that in my health and relationship goals.

In this time and age, the buzzword on everyone's lips is manifestation, synchronicity, and purpose. These are grandiose terms that evoke inspiration, but why is it that not everyone is living the life of their dreams? We live in a world where "fake it until you make it" is seen as the norm. Yes, the universe gives you what you are, not what you want. But, what happens when you can't even fake it? When you can't believe in yourself?

Have you ever tried to convince yourself that you're thin, even though your clothes are tight and uncomfortable? Or that you're happy, even though a part of you is constantly nagging that nothing ever works out for you? You might be an expert in manifestation, but if you're too attached to the outcome, all your programming becomes negated.

The result? Nothing changes.

This is where the lack mentality creeps in. When we're so fixated on the end goal, we forget that there might be something even better waiting for us. We forget that true manifestation comes from becoming the person we want to be, not just trying to enact it with good intentions.

Grabbing, pushing, pulling and remaining stuck. Stuck because you forget that your subconscious runs on autopilot, that there is already a program running that first needs to be overridden, so you can create from a space of safety and satisfaction and not desperately holding onto the end result.

When I started writing this book, I was in that same space. I knew the concepts, I knew what my end goal was but it was so hard for me to trust the process and be open to becoming it.

So if you would like something amazing to happen, read on, as these are such simple tools that I came across that changed my life. I don't believe in faking it, which means already you are not it. Trust the methods, apply them and slowly see the shifts. No transformation is an overnight success, some shifts happen in 2 seconds while for some it may be weeks or months. But the shifts are guaranteed. I have seen that in my life, I have taught many and as I finish writing this book, it's a confirmation that ascension is close.

My journey to personal growth and self-discovery began several years ago, but it was at my lowest point that I experienced a significant acceleration in my growth. It's a common theme among coaches, authors, and successful individuals- transformations often happen at a breaking point. The "dark night of the soul" is a term used to describe the moment when you feel like there's no way out, when you've hit rock bottom and nothing or no one can help you.

For me, it was a time when my entire life was falling apart. I was questioning everything I had worked for, believed in, and created. I wondered if I even deserved any of it. I was at a stage where I couldn't bring myself to get out of bed, and giving presentations to my clients was a source of overwhelming fear and insecurity. My dream company, which I had built from the ground up over the course of 15 years, was now a source of doubt and self-doubt.

One night, I completely broke down. I was inconsolable, and the tears flowed easily and non-stop. I got on my knees and asked whoever was "up there" to show me the way out of this darkness. After hours of crying, I went to bed at 8 PM and passed out from pure exhaustion. That was my "dark night of the soul", the moment when I realized that I needed to make a change and find my way back to the light.

Prologue

Embrace The Journey: A Love Letter To Life

As l close my eyes and dream,

A vision of a brighter future gleams. Where every sunrise is more magical, And every moment, more magical.

l travel to exotic lands,

And bask in beauty that's beyond grand.

l live in the moment, with love and grace, With joy in my heart, and a smile on my face.

Each day is a new adventure, a chance to explore, To create a reality that l've never seen before.

With a heart full of love, and a spirit so free, l immerse myself in life, and all it can be.

l am in love with life, and all its beauty,

And l know that the world is full of endless possibilities. With a single thought, l can change my fate,

And see a brighter future, one that's truly great.

We all have a calling, a purpose that we are meant to fulfill in this lifetime. For some, it is a whisper that they can barely hear, while for others it is a roar that demands their attention. But no matter how it presents itself, the path to true transformation and fulfillment is not an easy one.

Along the way, we encounter countless obstacles and distractions that threaten to derail our progress and discourage us from moving forward. We are plagued by self-doubt, fear, and the temptation to settle for less than what we are capable of. It is easy to give in to these obstacles and retreat back into our comfort zones, but that only leads to a life of regret and missed opportunities.

In "Ascension Codes", Manisha reveals the secrets to breaking through these obstacles and reaching the summit of our potential. With her expertise in yoga, meditation, and mindset coaching, she provides practical tools and techniques for unlocking our full power and becoming the best version of ourselves. Through her own story of personal growth and transformation, she shows us that when we can't fake it, we can learn how to become it.

Join Manisha on this journey of self-discovery and find the courage to rise above the challenges that are holding you back. Open your mind, heart, and soul, and discover the ascension codes that will unleash your full potential and guide you on the path to true transformation.

Fast forward

A Cry For Help

"I need your help, promise me you'll help me understand how to get unstuck and figure out my life."

"I need your help, can I connect with you to learn how to really transform my body, life, and soul?"

"I need help with my purpose." "I need to find myself."

"Can you please help me, I am lost."

"I want what you have, I think it's amazing. Change me, please!" "Just guide me, I'll do whatever it takes. I'll even do yoga if you want me to."

These are just a few of the calls I've received in recent months.

The last one came from someone close to me, and it made me pause. Suddenly, everyone seemed to be seeking my guidance on how they could change their lives, bodies, or purposes. The roles had suddenly been reversed.

As I reflected on these calls for help, I realized that we are all searching for something- be it a change in our bodies, our lives, or our sense of purpose. We all want to feel fulfilled and happy, but sometimes, we just don't know how to get there. That's where this book comes in. Through the pages of this book, l hope to guide you on your own journey of self-discovery and transformation.

As a lifelong seeker of personal growth, I've been on a journey to uncover the meaning of my life. I was drawn to courses, certifications, and any other tools that would help me find my purpose and make a meaningful impact on the world. Little did I know that my purpose was hiding in plain sight all along, buried within the very question I was asking: how can I help others become their best selves?

It wasn't an easy road to get here, of course. There's always a turning point, a moment of pain or hardship that propels us deeper into the depths of self-discovery. For me, that moment came during what felt like the darkest night of my soul. But when morning came, I woke up to a newfound appreciation for the opportunities that each day holds for growth and transformation. And so, my journey of personal development truly began.

With tear-streaked cheeks and a puffy face, I found myself at a turning point. I realized that I had the power to change my life for the better. So, I took a deep breath, grabbed my journal, and set to work charting out my intentions for every aspect of my life: health, career, relationships, love, experiences, purpose, and life vision. I poured my heart into it, delving deep into each category, determined to erase any limiting beliefs or negative programming that stood in the way of my true life vision.

Rewind

I love rewinds, because they put everything in perspective, maybe somewhere my journey will resonate with yours and it'll spark something. So here we go.

Happiness, positivity, and a great upbringing - I had it all. Or so I thought. Little did I know, my belief system was holding me back from reaching my full potential. My two biggest pain points - my body size and love life - seemed to be always getting in the way of my happiness. As an athletic and active yoga instructor, I couldn't seem to shake off my lingering struggles with my body size. Despite being strong, I felt frustrated with my inability to achieve the lean physique I desired. Meanwhile, in my love life, I found myself constantly attracting players, unavailable partners, and drama-filled relationships. No matter how hard I tried, I couldn't seem to manifest the peaceful and fulfilling romance I wanted. But through these struggles, I realized that the areas of my life that felt unfulfilling were the areas where I needed to do some deeper self-reflection and growth. It was time to delete any limiting programming and bring my vision for my life into focus.

I have come to understand that there are usually 3 things we as humans struggle with, relationships/love, health or finances. If you think back in your life or others, you will notice any of us stressing about either of these three. It's a human thing.

I had always known that I was an emotional person. I would cry at both happy and sad movies, and I would get invested in people so quickly that I would often lose myself in the process. This was a result of being an empath - people are drawn to that energy because they need something, and as long as I was still searching for my own personal reality, I would continue to give and give.

But my heartbreak was a wake-up call. It was time for me to do some serious soul-searching and reflection, to understand who I truly was and what I wanted out of life. It was time for me to take control of my own personal reality and create a life that was fulfilling and meaningful to me.

I delved into self-discovery, exploring my values, my passions, and my beliefs. I read books, attended workshops, and spoke to people who had been through similar experiences. I journaled my thoughts and feelings, and I meditated to connect with my inner self.

And slowly but surely, I began to see the transformation taking place within me. I became more confident in who I was, I learned to set boundaries, and I started to manifest a life that was in alignment with my values and desires. I no longer felt like a giver, but a powerful creator of my own reality.

It was a long and winding journey, but it was worth it. I am now living a life that is authentic and true to who I am, and I am grateful for that heartbreak that sparked the transformation.

Now that's the thing with understanding, there has to be a willingness to learn, I made it into a science project, reading researching, just going deeper into various aspects.

Some said, inner child healing, I totally understand that, but how the hell do you know what went wrong when I was 7 years old, or really what did I learn in the womb.

I tried thinking back on what I might possibly be blaming this on.

Funnily, I figured that my parents are awesome and did a really great job, my relatives loved me, so what the hell happened to the inner child. By the end of it, I decided I'd just send love to my inner child and hope she settles down a bit, because maybe she's just a child who is into tantrums. So mostly it was me hugging my tiny self.

I delved deeper into my childhood, searching for the root of my pain, but what I found was love and acceptance from my family. And yet, even with a sheltered upbringing, one in three children still suffer from sexual abuse. I realized that pain is inevitable, but it's up to me whether I want to be stuck in that suffering forever.

So, I made a choice. I took the time to fully resolve the part of me that blamed myself, accepted that I cannot change the past, and took full responsibility for my future. I moved from victimhood to empowerment, from pain to power.

It's important to talk about these things, because society often refuses to acknowledge the pain and trauma that we endure. But we must have the courage to face our fears head-on and confront our past in order to heal and move forward. My journey may help you do the same.

The fear of being judged, being wronged or even re-living the past. But how will you clean the house, when you dust everything under the carpet. The garbage will come back one way or the other. Better to have the courage to look it in the eye, say thank you for showing up and move forward. Maybe my journey will help you see the fears head on and acknowledge, accept and recover.

Tarot readings, meditations, I left no stone unturned, because I wanted to know how I could manifest a perfect way bypassing my old programming. That's when slowly the magic started unwinding and bam the law of attraction suddenly comes into focus.

The law of attraction basically works on "**you attract what your reality it**". If your self-talk or subconscious reality is that you are not lucky, you are not lucky, if you believe you are strong, you are strong. If you believe you are helpless, well, then you are.

Law of attraction basically works on "you attract what your reality it". If your self-talk or subconscious reality is that you are not lucky, you are not lucky, if you believe you are strong, you are strong. If you believe you are helpless, well, then you are.

Law of attraction has an offshoot which is called the law of assumption. Assumption because, you assume a reality, it is true if you believe it. Right, wrong, good or bad, doesn't matter, it's what you believe, so it is.

Law of assumption will guide all your actions. If you look at your life right now and take a moment to think, you will see the evidence all around you.

Universe does not give you what you want, it gives you

what you are!

Our wants and desires might be very relevant but if you feel that you do not deserve what you are asking for, you will not receive.

You desire a new job, while every day you hate going to work. You desire money, but feel you never get it, it's so hard to make money.

Whatever you are, is what you will receive, it's called unconditional love. It doesn't judge anything as good or bad, it just is. The universe loves you like that, whatever you are asking from you will keep getting it, whether its in your best interest or not.

That's where the entire precinct of fake it till you make it comes through. It's a play on the law of assumption.

We have heard of it, we've experienced it and as you read on it'll start becoming more evident as you reflect on your life.

Now here is the thing, if someone has a hard time feeling loved, you ask them to fake being unconditionally loved, I found that hard to digest. You tell someone who is struggling with weight to believe you are in perfect shape, again that's hard. When it came to the idea of fake it till you make it, I just couldn't stomach it. Though I understood the gist, the law of attraction basically delivers to you what you are. Your wishes and wants will take a backseat if you are not at a frequency of abundance. So here I was armed with that knowledge but totally clueless on how to get it done.

While in my various in-depth studies, I did come across practices and modalities that really can switch your reality. And yes these worked for me and I'm sharing those in case you would like to switch up yours.

Whatever reality is for you, maybe it's amazing, it's a dream come true or perhaps there are areas in your life that could be better. The methods work anyway, there is no starting benchmark. These are so easy and effortless that you won't even know you are doing anything until you see how the world starts shifting for you.

So if you are ready to not fake it but become it, I would say read on!

It All Starts with You

Who is the most important character of your story, YOU

The money, the love, the life, the purpose, it typically all boils down to how you are doing.

Do you feel you deserve the life that you keep wanting?

For me, there was this inner part of me that just decided I cannot make a good choice in men, it kept running in my internal software that I wasn't enough. Somewhere deep down in our psychological system, we have a program running on auto-pilot. That auto-pilot program decides how we show up. For e.g., if you decide to quit a job you hate, the first thing that rears its head is, how the hell will you pay the bills. Will you even get a better one? Or when you decide to go and make that video on social media, suddenly the thoughts like what would "they" say. I'll look like a fool, I have nothing good to say.

When you want to ask for something for yourself, the thoughts could be that I sound greedy, I should just not speak.

Here are some of the programs that run on auto-pilot-

Money can't buy happiness.

Poor but proud.

Nothing ever works out for me.

If it doesn't kill you, it makes you stronger.

Iam not worthy of love.

I am not important enough.

These are auto-pilot program thoughts that we've been fed through our lives. It could be from our family, friends or even as a subconscious belief.

These are really not very empowering. The most common is in finances, struggling to make ends meet doesn't leave you empowered, far less you being of any help to others.

That little sound in the background is your belief system. I call it your mental Netflix, the movie that's just playing in the background.

Let's just say the voices will remain but your belief system will decide your next action, whether you go on that stage, whether you make that choice for your career, or in love.

The voices in your head are meant to be your safety net, our mind tries to save us from anything that might have a negative outcome, because it knows what negative is for you. It's the purpose of your mind to be negative. For eons, we needed that defense system to stay alive in the caves, but now that guiding system is telling you to not leave the job that sucks, the relationship that is not good for you. The re-wiring will show your Inner Guidance that there may be a positive out of it.

These beliefs are ingrained and yes that's the inner child they were talking about, it's there, but again you don't have to go looking into finding out what happened, but instead override them.

When a virus attacks your system, you don't go looking for where it came from, you put an anti-virus system in place. It's quite the same, we are a machinery of magic yet we play small, because we are not anchoring ourselves to the positives.

So instead of looking for my internal viruses, I simply decided I needed a mindset upgrade. Most issues come from self-love and abandonment beliefs. That's a good place to start anyway, an extra dose of self-love can't go waste.

Once you decide that you are the most important person in your life, your happiness stops being dependent on others. Your needs and wants literally just become play. It's like when you are a baby, it's predestined that you will be fed, clothed, put to bed and get love.

You are not fighting for any of it, because now that you will have systems in place that will not attract anything unwanted towards you.

So, that became my system, me being my focal point, all the love and care I poured into others, I decided I wanted that for myself.

Self-love concept is more than a physical upgrade or a salon visit, yes those work too but we are talking about re-writing your software. So start with the basic coding. I started with I am….

Every night, I decided to write a love letter to myself, which started with Iam amazing..

Every night, I decided to write a love letter to myself, which started with Iam amazing.

Embarking on this is hard, it's hard because it feels narcissistic, we hate praising ourselves right? WRONG! It all starts with you, if you cannot be your biggest cheerleader, don't expect the world to be.

It all starts with you, if you cannot be your biggest cheerleader, don't expect the world to be First put your own oxygen mask before helping others, you cannot help others if you yourself are not safe and supported.

The exercise was fairly simple, I started with writing Iam amazing because (start with basic) I showed up for work, Iam amazing because I moved 10k steps, and so on. Write at least twenty, it's a process.

It's so simple yet it shifts something deep inside. When you internalize your validation, you don't care about the external environment.

The next step was how to make it stick, after about a week of this everyday writing, they became my auto-pilot responses. I prefer writing, there is a pen to paper brain connection that cannot be replaced. A few weeks into the practice, I started putting this on my screensaver, then as a wallpaper and even as reminders.

Iam amazing. Iam love. Iam powerful. Iam joyful. Iam spectacular. Iam supported. Iam loved. I am worthy. iam abundant and on and on.

As many as you can come up with. Just keep adding to the list, and read it every hour. When as a child, you were trying to commit to memory or understand a difficult chapter for exams you read it again and again until each paragraph was committed to memory. Think of it as exam prep and give it your

100 percent. This is your preparation for acing in the exams life will be hurling at you.

Now there will be days when you will not feel much empowered, those are the days you write 50 I am.

That's the lifeboat. When you are down, that inner guidance needs you to give it something to empower you. Don't miss a day of doing this, it's going to prove to be your life jacket in all situations.

The shifts that you notice are, you will reach out to the most resonating Iam you created when you are in a situation. Your mind will start shifting, which in turn will shift your reality.

When you become your favorite cheerleader that's when the world will cheer for you. Some call it confidence, some say it's your reality, I would say this is the bare minimum you need, to make your life magical. The more grounded you are in your reality, the better friends you'll have. You will notice more opportunities, you will definitely be more likable. You don't need to know how, just trust that you need this as your anchor and practice.

Now just doing it for a day or week will not be enough, our programs run for years, if you tend to get in your head, just write it on paper 2O times. We are here to have the best life, then why wouldn't you want you up-level your beliefs to feel worthy of that life. It will work only if you do it. Step out of your comfort zones and get to work. It's time to create a better reality.

Breakdowns Are Breakthroughs

Sometimes it takes an overwhelming breakdown to have an epic breakthrough

Now this maybe a chapter that your mind will want to shut out, but hold on. We all have had a hard time in life and usually you'll notice you come out better. We started with the first exercise to pave an easier way of navigating life lessons.

Life is full of twists and turns, but that's what makes it all the more thrilling. Let's take a walk down memory lane to a time when you planned the perfect picnic. The sun was shining, your friends and family were eager to enjoy the great outdoors with you. But, as luck would have it, just as you arrived, the skies opened up and rain came pouring down. What a bummer, right? Not so fast! This is where you get to turn lemons into lemonade. No amount of complaining or cursing will make the rain go away, but with a little creativity, you can still have a blast. Maybe you have a raindrop picnic in your car, play a muddy game, or simply find a tree to huddle under.

The point is, even though things didn't go as planned, you still had a memorable time. Embrace the Adventure!

And what about the heartbreak? We've all been there, falling head over heels for someone who we thought was the one. But when it ends abruptly, it can leave us feeling like life has dealt us a cruel blow. But this is exactly when you need to call upon all the resilience and strength you've built up. In the midst of your pain, search for one good thought that brings a glimmer of joy. Remember, life is a journey, and every twist and turn is just another opportunity to make memories that will last a lifetime.

The real tests come when the emotions are too high. When you are very attached to the outcome. This is the time when you need to use all your training. At our lowest point, look for a thought that feels good.

Feel the anger, feel the frustration, do not ever try to hold it in, scream, shout, cry. When you exhaust the feelings start digging in for a memory that feels good.

This is not a diversion of pain, no net-flixing here or

binge eating.

No we will not be indulging in numbing the pain. Instead we are going to feel it, even if it hurts, let it all surface and then find that good feeling thought or go outside and play, walk, move.

It's hard at first, but fully accepting how you feel helps unfold the wounding. And it's not make-believe, it's basically the cycle of life.

When you ask for an upgrade from a situation, something will change, something will shift and you may not be prepared. The superpower is knowing that better things come right after.

The superpower is knowing that better things come right after.

From Oprah Winfrey to J.K. Rowling, history is littered with examples of individuals who faced seemingly insurmountable obstacles, but still managed to rise above them and achieve greatness. The key to their success was the way they looked at the challenges they faced. Rather than being defeated by setbacks, they saw them as opportunities for growth and transformation.

As you strive for a better life, be prepared for changes. Some people may have to leave your life, old fears may surface, but that's because you're being upgraded to the next level. When you manifest something bigger, the universe may show you the areas where you need to work on yourself, so that you can become the person who deserves the upgrade. If you don't believe you're worthy of having your needs met, you'll keep getting the same results. But once you realize that you deserve better, everything will change.

Remember, when things fall apart, they're simply making way for something new and better. The old is being transformed into the new. So embrace the journey, even if it includes a "tower moment" as its referred to in tarot cards. Know that every challenge is an opportunity to become stronger and better.

What really helps here is, when you are feeling low, when sad emotions are running strong, that's when maximum change is due, so take a moment to feel them. We are often asked to not cry, not feel bad by everyone around us. Instead I would say feel them fully, let them wash over you 100%, as emotions are human experiences. They might not be desirable because sometimes they hurt but acknowledge that and let them show up. Don't be afraid of them, they are a part of you. At this time, just hug yourself and start rewriting your next best intention.

And once you have stayed for some time in those emotions, its time to move on. Its time to snap out of it. You are not meant to wallow for days, its an emotion that can be fleeting, it could last a day too but then you need to get to work, take responsibility to feel better and give it all.

Stop listening to sad songs instead switch the playlist to happier songs. If tears fall, let them. Get off the couch and start moving. Get on your feet and dance.

At this time, just hug yourself and start rewriting your best intentions Stop listening to sad songs instead switch the playlist to happier songs If tears fall, let them Get off the couch and start moving Get on your feet and dance.

Dance like no one is watching, dance like you are in a trance.

Next, find that next happy feeling, it could be watching your young happy photos or memories from a holiday. Find that happy thought which will start shifting your reality.

Next, learn to breathe to LET IT GO. Sit with your eyes closed, one hand on your chest, the other on your belly. Breathe in through the nose for 4 counts, hold the breath for 4 counts and breathe out through the mouth for 8 counts. Breathe in calm, breathe out anger. Breathe in peace, breathe out abandonment, breathe in love, breathe out grudges. Letting go is longer so your out-breath is longer.

Breathe in peace, breathe out abandonment, breathe in love breathe out grudges Letting go is longer so your out-breath is longer.

When life presents its challenges, it can be easy to feel overwhelmed and defeated. But it's important to remember that the beauty of life is still yours to experience, and that you hold the power to elevate your spirit and find joy, even in tough times.

Here are a few simple steps that can help you do just that:

Embrace the power of movement: Dancing to a feel-good tune is a great way to lift your mood and get your body moving. When we dance, we release endorphins, the feel-good hormones that help us feel happier and more relaxed. So, turn up the music and get lost in the rhythm. Our bodies have innate wisdom, it already knows how to let loose. The best way to start is , start dancing alone. We tend to focus too much on what others may say or feel when we are in public, so create a space for YOU. This is a space where you will play the happiest song, close your eyes if you must and just let yourself move. We store emotions as energy and when we are undergoing some change, it tends to get stuck. Let it flow, let it move. Doing this right in the morning before you start your day is a great way to let loose. It is exhilarating, it is joyful. It may feel odd when you begin but you will see how magical your energy will be, soon, very soon.

Allow yourself to feel: Sometimes we need to let out our emotions in order to feel better. Crying, screaming, or shouting can be cathartic and help relieve the stress and tension that we're holding onto. Don't be afraid to let yourself feel, and remember that it's okay to be vulnerable and express your emotions. We are often told that stop moping over a loss, "get over it", dont cry, etc etc. Its usually uncomfortable for most of us to acknowledge any emotion openly, because we are conditioned to be in control. But emotions are free and need to be expressed, when you are hurt, vent it out first, come back into balance with your own inner world and then try and resolve. Emotional intelligence is all about learning to embrace and not react.

When we get hurt, its usually a boundary has been breached. First, come to terms with what was breached. Get acquainted with the source behind the emotion, let it well up to its maximum capacity and then CHOOSE to let it go. Choose to feel, then choose to let go. That's you in control.

The more you hold back the emotions, the bigger will be the outburst later. Emotions are not good or bad. It's easy to label certain emotions as negative, but they all serve a purpose. Anger can motivate us to make positive changes, sadness can help us process grief, and fear can keep us safe. By paying attention to our own emotions, we can better understand what triggers them and learn to manage them more effectively. The result is greater resilience and well-being. Another emotion that I'm usually being blamed for is joy and happiness. I would hear a lot of people say " in your perfect world…" and usually it isn't meant as a complement. We tend to label someone who is happy to be less committed. Sometimes, happy-go-lucky becomes a negative connotation. We have to learn to be happy when we feel it. It does not need to be a great achievement that we celebrate, it is just a state of being. I personally love to be in awe, awe of nature, what I can learn and how I feel, its such a wonder. Start by being aware of what brings you awe, start by being aware of how you feel. Through the day, check-in multiple times on how you are feeling, acknowledge it. I play a game where I simply ask myself "what am i feeling in that moment" and just repeat " Iam feeling…" No judgment, no questions, just a space to feel.

Practice self-care: Giving yourself a comforting hug can be a simple yet powerful way to show yourself some love and compassion. This physical touch can help release oxytocin, the hormone associated with feelings of love and connection, and make you feel more relaxed and calm. The science behind hugging suggests that hugging a person for over 10 secs can release a lot of stress. Hugging yourself can invoke a feeling of self-love. A simple practice I learned from Paul Mckenna, the renowned hypnotherapist is based on the same principle. When you feel triggered or have a memory you are trying to embrace just cross your arms across the chest and gently stroke each arm. Close your eyes, breathe deeply, in through he nose, out through the mouth and keep stroking your arms lovingly. This simple gesture can get you into a deeper level of calm and self-love.

Take deep breaths: Deep breathing is a great tool for releasing tension and calming the mind. Take a few deep breaths, inhaling slowly and exhaling slowly, and focus on the sensation of air moving in and out of your body. This can help you feel more relaxed and centered, and can be done anywhere, anytime, to help you find peace and tranquility. In my many years of yoga practice, we are taught how breath is the source of life. You notice how the breath becomes shallow and faster when you are angry or stressed, while it slows down completely when you are peaceful and happy. The breathing pattern can be changed at will to activate what you want to feel and how you want to experience life. I personally love to start my day with box breaths, that is making a box with a count of 5 breaths. This pattern activates the parasympathetic nervous system bringing instant calm. When you are in a state of agitation or heightened emotion, simply breathe in through the nose to a count of 5, hold the breath for 5 counts, out through the mouth for 5 counts and hold for 5. Repeat this multiple times for 5X5X5X5. Even if you are in control most of the time, try this breathing pattern to improve focus and improve your performance.

Remember, even during the toughest of times, you hold the power to feel better. By embracing these simple steps, you can elevate your spirit, cultivate positive emotions, and find joy in your life.

Your external surroundings may be challenging, but

it's up to you how quickly you bounce back. Pain is inevitable, but suffering is a choice. We often prolong our suffering by reliving past memories or worrying about the future. Instead, choose to focus on a brighter future and the joy of being alive with those who love you. Choosing to see the positive can have a powerful impact on your well-being, turning a breakdown into a breakthrough.

Breakdowns can be tough, but they also hold immense potential for growth and transformation. When we face challenges and difficulties, it can be tempting to focus on the negative and dwell on the pain and suffering that we're experiencing. But we have a choice. We can choose to see these breakdowns not as obstacles, but as opportunities.

When we choose to see the positive in our challenges, we open ourselves up to a world of possibilities. By deciding to choose a happier future, we give ourselves the power to create the life that we want. We can choose to focus on the good things in our lives, like the people who love us and the fact that we are alive and have the power to create change.

By choice we can tap into a powerful source of strength and resilience. We can harness the power of our thoughts and emotions to create a better reality for ourselves. By choosing to feel good, even in the face of difficulty, we open ourselves up to a world of positivity and hope.

It's important to remember that our thoughts and emotions have a direct impact on our lives. When we choose to focus on the negative, we invite more negativity and suffering into our lives. But when we choose to focus on the positive, we cultivate happiness, love, and joy. So, in the face of challenge, make the decision to choose a happier future and to see breakdowns as points of growth and transformation. Your future is in your hands, and the power to create it is within you.

Mini Soul Expansions

We are such amazing beings, the whole point of humans having feelings is to be able to live beautiful experiences.

Every day, every second, life is giving us mini moments of expansion. Expansion of feelings, lifestyle, and expectations, you name it.

A lot of us look at people who have a lot of money and say "Oh they are born into wealth". Or people who have epic experiences, some say "they don't have to work and make a living, so they can afford to".

Whenever we see something that we remotely desire, like the perfect figure, a legendary life, we kill that inner desire by attaching a low remark to it.

The usual ones would sound like-

Gorgeous figure - she doesn't have a job and family to juggle, so she has time to workout.

Amazing love life - they have nothing else to do.

Epic travel pictures - probably has too much money to spend, and of course doesn't work 9 to 5.

Every time we see something we would like to have, we try to justify why we don't have. I have no time, I'm overworked, I don't know how, and my life is complicated. Some even dislike it because something within them hates that we can't have it. There is separation, there is jealousy, and there is a negative emotion of lack.

So each moment of life, you are being given a chance for mini expansion. Instead of judging the experience or the quality, **take a moment to reflect on how it would feel if you had it.**

The more negative emotion that comes through you, the more separation you have from that desire.

Freedom becomes having no responsibilities, love becomes putting on a show, great health becomes having too much time.

Instead what if you take these micro moments to really feel what you would like.

These are your micro -mediations for the moment. You are creating life on the go, each time you are thinking a thought, you are bringing it into motion, each time you are feeling, and you are activating the desire to have it.

These are your micro meditations in the moment. You are creating life on the go, each time you are thinking a thought, you are bringing it into motion, each time you are feeling, and you are activating the desire to have it.

So instead of feeling the lack of it, why not embody it. When you see something desirable, why not have it.

The power of our thoughts, feelings, and beliefs is a well- documented phenomenon in both spiritual and scientific circles. According to quantum physics, our reality is created through the lens of our perception, and our perceptions are shaped by our thoughts, feelings, and beliefs. This means that, to a large extent, our reality is a reflection of our inner world. Buddha said, 'We are what we think. All that we are arises with our thoughts. With our thoughts, we make the world.'

Studies have shown that our thoughts and feelings have a direct impact on our biology, influencing the release of hormones and neurotransmitters that can impact our mood and well-being. When we focus on positive thoughts and feelings, we activate the body's 'relaxation response,' promoting feelings of calm and contentment. On the other hand, when we dwell on negative thoughts and feelings, we activate the 'stress response,' leading to feelings of anxiety and distress.

It's in this context that micro soul expansions become so important. These are the tiny moments in our day when we choose to focus on the good and bring it into our present moment. By doing so, we are planting the seeds of positivity and abundance in our minds, allowing them to grow and blossom into a beautiful reality.

As Wayne Dyer says, 'Change the way you look at

things and the things you look at change.'

As Wayne Dyer says, 'Change the way you look at things and the things you look at change '.

These micro meditations are a form of self-care that nourish the soul, helping us align with the reality we desire. By embodying the good we see in the world, we tap into the power of creation and manifestation, bringing more of what we want into our lives. So, the next time you feel yourself getting lost in negative thoughts and feelings, take a moment to stop and focus on the good.

I live my day like that. If I see something beautiful, I literally feel excited about it and voice it in my head "what would it take for something so amazing to have happen for me".

Suddenly, the fear of missing out on the experience turns into embodying it. You chose to have a good experience in your life.

Suddenly the fear of missing out on that experience turns into you embodying it. You chose to have a good experience

This works like a charm, we spend all day thinking about our work, our responsibilities, and our limitations but if you did take out these micro moments to actually voice your desires, it'll change and shift your reality so fast. Your brain and thoughts are sacred, think of them like tofu, now marinate your brain with love and the best ingredients, the dish will obviously turn out delicious. Go on a brain diet, every negative emotion is overridden with a positive embodiment. Strave the negative, feed the positive.

You see someone wearing clothes that you like, envision and see if you like what that looks like. You see a relationship that you like, try to embody that. It's similar to trying new trends, you like something and say yes I would like that. Feel the feelings of having it, how would it feel on your skin, what would you smell, what would it bring into your life. There are so many chances in a day that you get to shift into a new expansion, give yourself that time and space to feel them. Envision, engage your feelings, love it and become it.

You are making a moment to moment choice of up-leveling your life. You are inviting new experiences, new abundance, and new ways of being. You already have the visual stimulus, all you need to do is embody it by asking what it would take for you to have that in your life.

You are making a moment to moment choice of up- leveling your life. You are inviting new experiences, new abundance, and new ways of being. You already have the visual stimulus, all you need to do is embody it by asking what it would take for you to have that in your life.

Our subconscious is beautiful, it's magic. When you ask that question, and have the real desire to have that, it automatically starts to scout how to make it happen for you. The key is desire, you actually have to feel it and follow it with the question, so you start seeing possible answers to it. When you ask a question, it is impossible for your brain to not come up with an answer. Now if you switch the questions to what can bring you what you desire, wouldnt it be easier to create.

In my life, when I started doing this, I asked about

getting to my ideal body and within a few weeks I came across everything I needed in terms of a mindset shift, a nutrition upgrade to a workout upgrade that made it happen within a few months.

Energy flows where desire goes, so top it with things that you DO WANT instead of filling your mind with something that doesn't grow you.

I believe that having a consistent meditation practice is amazing but being able to get into that state of calm and joy, minute to minute, in everyday hustle is even better. The micro meditation will allow you to switch from a negative to a positive mindset within that time instead of waiting to process it when you get back on your meditation cushion.

You are living in the now, so start making choices in the now. By embracing the philosophy of micro-soul expansion, you are choosing to live life differently. You are choosing to break free from the limiting beliefs and negative patterns that hold you back and instead adopt a proactive approach to personal growth and self-discovery. The idea behind this concept is that by continuously debugging and refining your thoughts, feelings, and beliefs, you can create a life that aligns with your deepest desires.

Research has shown that our thoughts have a powerful impact on our emotions and behaviors. In fact, a study by the National Institutes of Mental Health found that individuals who consistently practiced positive self-talk and affirmations experienced significant reductions in anxiety and depression symptoms. This highlights the importance of monitoring your thoughts and replacing negative ones with positive, empowering ones.

Moreover, a report by the World Health Organization states that stress, which is often a result of negative thought patterns, is the leading cause of long-term health problems, including heart disease and stroke. By practicing micro-soul expansions, you are reducing stress and anxiety by continuously refining your thought processes, and thus, reducing the risk of developing these health problems.

In conclusion, debugging on the go, rather than proofreading at the end of the project, is a more efficient and effective approach to personal growth and self-discovery. By embracing micro-soul expansions, you are taking control of your thoughts, beliefs, and emotions and empowering yourself to create a life that aligns with your desires. Choose to live in the moment, make each thought, feeling, and action count and enjoy the journey of self-discovery.

The mind is a canvas, and every thought is a brushstroke, transform it to see opportunities for growth, joy, and fun.

Ask Better Questions

Why Is This Happening To Me?

Why can't I ever find happiness? Why do I keep making mistakes? Why why why?

Basic questions that we tend to ask. Something unpleasant happens, why I always feel targeted. Someone breaks your heart, I am broken.

You are exactly what you ask for and probably just receive more of it. We are always trying to understand why something bad happened to us, while most of us wouldn't even give a thought on why something good happened. You don't question the good then why question the bad. Now good or bad is relative here, a point of reference.

We are experiential beings, and from each experience we will shape our thoughts, our beliefs and ways of being. When something undesirable happens, a loop in the thought process is activated, where our dear friend, the subconscious is looking at possible ways to avoid this emotional threat in the future.

Interesting point here is the law of attraction, when you keep asking why something undesirable is happening, you have the highest emotion of creation and you activate a string of unpleasant scenarios.

Ever heard of the domino effect, when one thing falls all start falling, that's what happens, you invite in a major windfall of like experiences.

When you are experiencing a beautiful moment, you will notice how everything is full of pleasantness. When you go on the perfect honeymoon, the weather is right, the food is great, you meet the most amicable people, you have the best photos, and it goes on. Your reaction to a situation invites a string of like experiences.

When you are having a spell of bad luck, everything appears to be falling apart, until you decide to switch it.

Here comes the art of becoming. The art of asking the

right questions or learning how to switch the situation to a desirable one.

So instead of asking why it is happening to me, change the narrative to a more positive one, change it to what would it take……

For example, if I lose my luggage instead of asking the usual why is it happening to me, I'd rather switch it to what would it take for me to have my luggage back. Or even better what would it take to have my luggage back in time so I can continue having the best travel experience.

Asking this about 2O/3O times with conviction and it can switch the situation in the most magical way.

The key here is to really believe that it can happen. Bring in the hope and knowingness in your questions, so that it really sets forth the movement towards desire.

Another switch phrase to ask a better question is what do I need to become. We discussed how life is always trying to get you to up level, you can call it getting older, wiser, whatever, and it's always trying to get you to a level where you feel better.

The better question when you feel you haven't achieved your heart's desire is to ask, what do I need to become. It is commonly believed that putting in more time and effort at work will lead to more wealth and financial stability, and that giving more love will result in receiving more in return. However, studies and observations have shown that this is not necessarily the case. The rich, for instance, often have a unique mindset and way of being that attracts wealth to them, rather than them putting in more hours at work. This is supported by the concept of "the law of attraction," which posits that we attract what we embody and believe in.

Additionally, research has shown that simply working out more does not guarantee physical fitness. Giving more love does not get you more love. These realizations lead us to question what it is we truly need to become in order to achieve our desired outcomes.

Asking better questions can be a powerful tool in

re-programming our minds to see everything as an opportunity for growth, joy, and fulfillment. Instead of asking why a situation is happening to us, we can ask, "What do I need to become to have epic health?" or "What do I need to become to experience abundance in wealth?" By asking these questions regularly, we shift our focus from external circumstances to our own internal state and beliefs, which can have a significant impact on our lives.

The popular phrase "fake it until you make it" also highlights the importance of embodying the mindset and beliefs of those who have already achieved what we desire. It's not always easy, especially when faced with difficulties, but by consistently aligning our thoughts and beliefs with what we wish to achieve, we can attract the desired outcomes into our lives.

Patric Grover, the multi-millionaire would ask the question as a "how" instead of why, he would simply journal in his notebook 30-50 times, asking how could he make 100 million in 1 year.

This process is similar, instead of asking a dis-empowering question of why is it happening to me, why do I have no money, why is my body like this, you start asking better questions of what would it take or how can you get that dream car (insert exact car here please), that dream home (insert exact no. of rooms n description please) or even that dream health.

The why is not even important, what's important is you now know what you want and you are triggering your brain to think of all possible ways to get you that goal. I would again like to reiterate here that while you sit in the beautiful questions, know that an answer is forthcoming, it might not be within 24hrs, but it will arrive. Start with small wins, they build confidence and then move on to bigger ones. The smaller wins you wouldn't be so attached to, so they'll be easier for your brain to solve.

Go on and write your beautiful questions. That's the action. Write down 10 of your desires as "what would it take", "what can i become" or how do I". This is not an overnight success, so you may need to repeat these for a few days. If you see success, celebrate the wins. Celebration brings in more wins.

Look for Neon Signs

Now that you asked for something, you believe its coming. You've done the work. You are absolutely sure how it will feel when you have it. All the questions have been asked, feelings captured, but the results are not showing up.

STOP.

Do not give up. Instead, raise the faith. Abraham Hicks calls it driftwood.

I love the concept. This phenomenon can also be applied to our thoughts and beliefs. Our minds are powerful instruments that can shape our reality. What we focus on, we attract. It's like a magnet, drawing experiences and situations towards us that align with our thoughts and beliefs.

Take for example, the concept of the blue car. When you think about a blue car, suddenly you start to see blue cars everywhere. This happens because your mind is actively looking for and paying attention to blue cars. You are, in essence, asking for them, and your mind is helping you find them.

The same goes for a purple dress. If you think about a purple dress, you start to see more people wearing purple. This is because your mind is directing your attention to the color purple and the people who are wearing it.

This is what is known as the law of attraction, and it is a powerful tool for shaping our experiences and reality. By focusing on the things we want, we can attract more of those experiences and situations into our lives.

The concept of driftwood is also a powerful metaphor for our journey through life. Just like driftwood can be a sign that the shore is getting closer, our thoughts and beliefs can serve as a roadmap for where we are heading. When we focus on positive thoughts and beliefs, we are more likely to attract positive experiences and situations. On the other hand, when we focus on negative thoughts and beliefs, we are more likely to attract negative experiences and situations.

So, next time you find yourself lost at sea, remember

to look for driftwood. It could be a sign that you're getting closer to shore and to the life you want to lead. And, if you're feeling lost in life, take a moment to reflect on your thoughts and beliefs. By focusing on the things you want, you can attract more of those experiences and situations into your life.

The Universe only brings you aspects of others that are active within you So everything that you're getting, from everyone you're getting it from, you're getting it as an indication of your vibration. 'Hi, I'm your Vibrational Indicator'. You only get back what you are giving out vibrationally.

You're like my piece of driftwood in the ocean. Indicating to me that land is getting closer - Abraham-Hicks

You asked for a new job and boom, your friend comes running to you with excitement, telling you about an amazing opportunity they just landed. That, my friend, is your driftwood. It's the sign that you are aligned with your desires. The universe is constantly giving you clues and signs to show you what you're attracting.

And it's not just about the job, you asked for a better relationship, and suddenly all your social media feeds are overflowing with happy couples. That's your driftwood, the signs that you're on the right track.

Nothing takes time, it just takes alignment. When I was manifesting financial abundance, I kept meeting like-minded individuals and hearing stories of their breakthroughs. Instead of feeling discouraged and wondering why it wasn't happening for me, I chose to focus on the signs that it was happening.

The key is to steer your inner guidance system towards celebrating others' wins, so it can show up for you too. Trust in the universe's timing, and keep an eye out for your driftwood. It's always there, guiding you towards your desires.

Think of driftwood as the little nudges or hints that the universe is sending your way, telling you that you're on the right track, close to getting what you want. But what if the driftwood you're seeing isn't what you want? Let's say you're surrounded by negative gossip, drama, and unhappy stories. This is your cue to change your thought patterns. The things you see and experience in the world around you are a direct reflection of what's going on in your inner world. If you want something different to show up in your life, you need to change your inner world first.

So, here's what to do: take note of the driftwood you're seeing, express gratitude for it, and celebrate the wins of others that align with your goals. When you're feeling down and feel like your wishes are taking too long to come true, remember to be patient. The universe has its own timeline, but if you keep focusing on what you want and delete any thoughts of lack, you'll start seeing positive driftwood everywhere.

Any thought that stems from lack, low vibe or negativity, mentally say DELETE to it. Do this as many times as a negative thought rears its head. You can even call out CANCEL. With this process you are gently guiding your inner subconscious to let go of thoughts that are not empowering or do not fit what you desire.

And then....

Be patient!

Enjoy the process! Celebrate your journey!

I love to refer to these positive signs as "neon signs". These are the glowing signals that let you know you're on the right track and that your destination is getting closer every day. Just like the bright, eye-catching signs you see in a city, these neon signs are designed to catch your attention and keep you moving forward towards your goals.

Move to Groove

What will you find common in some of the most successful people, first they have great bodies, and they are agile, able to work through the day and have boundless energy.

Our bodies are intended to house our energy system, our life force. And energy is never static. What happens to a car when it's parked for too long, what happens to body parts that are not used? Because by the simple law of evolution, if there is no functionality, that part will be eliminated, it's the way our species progresses. Our body structure changed to adapt to walking on our legs instead of all fours. It's all about survival of the fittest.

This may sound like the usual "exercise is good for you" talk, but I want to reiterate it here.

Moving our body is essential for anyone who wants to up level in any area of your life. It's not about getting to a size, let's say it's more to do with getting your mind to work.

Our bodies are amazing, they run along with the magical system of our mind. Moving provides you with a burst of feel good hormones and neurotransmitters, the same guys who are involved in your emotions, your mood, your self-image, basically everything.

If you want to create a life filled with energy and vitality, you can't just sit idly and let stagnant energy take over. To truly thrive, you need to actively release the toxins and waste that accumulate in your body. One of the best ways to do this is through physical activity. It not only gets your sweat glands going, gets your muscles engaged, keeps your heart healthy, and nourishes your skin, but it also ignites changes in your life that you never thought were possible.

You might think that simply walking around or doing household chores counts as physical activity, but research has shown that it's important to have a different mindset about these activities. In a fascinating study, 12 female housekeeping staff were split into two groups. One group was told that their daily tasks were the equivalent of 2 hours of exercise, while the other group was simply told to keep up the good work. The results were striking. The group who believed their work was exercise lost twice as much weight as the other group in just a few short months. This study shows that it's not just the physical activity itself, but also how you perceive it, that makes a difference.

Next time you're walking around or doing household chores, take a moment to consciously recognize the effort you're putting in and the impact it's having on your body. By doing so, you'll be harnessing the power of your mind to achieve your goals and live a life filled with energy and vitality.

Physical activity is a crucial aspect of overall health and well-being. The human body requires a minimum of 8 minutes of high-intensity activity each day to function optimally. This does not have to be hours at the gym, but it should be enough to meet the body's basic needs.

When it comes to exercise, it's important to choose an activity that makes you feel happy and fulfilled, rather than simply following popular trends. This could be anything from pole dancing to yoga, weightlifting, or running. The key is to find an activity that keeps your body in motion and your happy hormones flowing.

There is ample scientific evidence that supports the benefits of physical activity on mental and physical health. In fact, some of the biggest stories of transformation start with a shift in the body, whether it's reaching a desired weight or simply feeling more confident in your skin. Movement releases endorphins that can raise your vibration and help you feel better both physically and mentally. Even a simple walk or jog can help shift your perspective and provide inspiration. So if you're feeling low or need a change of scenery, get up and get moving! Your body and mind will thank you.

Our bodies are designed to do multiple amazing things, so when I say health should be a first priority, it's stating the obvious. Don't wait for the perfect job, perfect vacation, and perfect situation to start stepping into the perfect body. Usually our motivation is getting into that wedding dress, looking good in a swimsuit or even a heartbreak to start focusing on our health. My belief is always be ready, because you want to be at your best when perfection shows up.

Incorporating physical activity into your daily routine can be a bit of a challenge, especially when you have a busy schedule and multiple responsibilities. But did you know that just a few minutes of high-intensity exercise each day can have a significant impact on your overall health and wellbeing? This is where the concept of "intermittent bursts of exercise" comes into play. By doing short, quick exercises throughout the day, you can reap the benefits of a traditional workout without sacrificing hours of your time.

Studies have shown that by incorporating short bursts of high-intensity exercise into your routine, you can increase your metabolism, reduce stress and anxiety, and burn fat. This approach to physical activity is a great way to maintain a healthy lifestyle, especially if you don't have the time or energy for a full workout. The best part is that you can do these exercises anywhere, at any time, without the need for any equipment. Some of the most effective exercises include jumping jacks, sit-ups, and push-ups.

If you're new to this concept, a simple routine to get started is 15 jumping jacks, 15 squats, and 15 push-ups, done three times a day. This will take you under 5 minutes and will provide a great boost to your metabolism, reduce stress, and help you burn fat. Regular physical activity is essential for maintaining good health, and incorporating short bursts of exercise into your daily routine can help you achieve this. By embracing this approach to fitness, you'll feel empowered and energized, and you'll be taking a major step towards a healthier, happier life.

The benefits of frequent and intentional movement go beyond just physical fitness. Incorporating short bursts of exercise throughout the day can have a profound impact on your mental health as well. Exercise has been shown to reduce symptoms of anxiety and depression, improve cognitive function, and increase feelings of happiness and well-being. When you engage in physical activity, your body releases endorphins, which are natural mood boosters.

Additionally, exercise has been shown to promote neuroplasticity, the brain's ability to change and adapt, which can improve brain function and memory. Furthermore, being in a constant state of movement, instead of just during structured workout sessions, can also lead to improved mindfulness and self-awareness. This mindfulness can then spill over into other areas of life, promoting a sense of calm and clarity. So not only will you be toning your muscles and burning fat, but you'll also be boosting your mood and cognitive abilities!

Here is a simple routine that you can follow to thrive a day-15 jumping jacks, 15 squats and 15 push-ups.

This will take under 5 minutes.

Start from wherever you are, if you can manage 5, start there, if you cannot do push-ups on the ground, start with wall push-ups. You do you, just move.

Maximizing the benefits of a daily workout, add that outdoor brisk walk. Especially in nature, it can do wonders for your physical and mental health. Set aside 21 minutes, crank up the pace, and hit the park or the nearest green space. Immerse yourself in the beauty of the natural surroundings, listen to your favorite tunes, sing at the top of your lungs, or catch up on your podcast. The combination of physical activity and fresh air will provide a boost to your energy levels, improve your mood, and lower stress levels.

But, don't just take my word for it, make the commitment to get out there and put in the work. The results will speak for themselves. In just one month, you'll start to see the positive changes in your body, mind, and overall well-being, even if you don't necessarily feel it at first. Trust the process and take that first step. Your health, happiness, and future self will thank you for it.

Be the Light

I had heard many stories about connecting to the light. Energy healers and meditators often teach white light meditation. Being the curious type, I decided to give it a try. As it turns out, we are all part of the collective universe and our lives are created by the vibrations we emit. Our current thoughts and feelings shape our future experiences. The universal law states that like attracts like, so if we want to attract better things, we need to start showing up better.

At first, I was only visualizing it and not sure how it worked, but now I know it does. I tried the meditation and then attempted to bend a metal spoon. To my surprise, the solid spoon became malleable with almost no effort. It was as if I was interacting with particles and they showed me how to bend and turn. Yes, it sounds completely batty, but then I bent a heavy duty metal serving spoon with almost zero strength. I went ahead and then got a fork. Same thing. I then tried to get deeper and started working on the spokes to flay them out and voila I had solid metals as fluid as clay.

Well, I had to try it to really understand if my mojo is working and I am a believer. Iam still not sure how it works. I do now know with practice of this super simple method, life becomes easier.

At the core, we are all oscillating, dancing particles. We interact with atoms and molecules every second, as we are made up of them. Although we appear solid, we are really dense energy forms. The theory that a heavy duty concrete bridge can be brought down if all the cars vibrate at the same frequency is real. I still don't know how it all works, but I am a believer in the power of white light meditation.

The white light is taught in yoga meditations as our connection to the divine. Now whether you like to call that god, higher power, universe, name is not as important as its existence. There is a power that is beyond our understanding that exists and holds the entire life system into balance. Nature, the environment, every system is designed impeccably to be in balance, the yin to the yang, the sun and the moon, birth and death.

The greatest creation is human, who is Co-creating with the universe.

Now we can continue to resist or rather let the flow guide us.

Resistance is what I call when you are feeling a negative emotion. Any lower vibrating emotions of anger, guilt, and shame are lower on the vibration scale. The higher vibrations are gratitude, joy, happiness, and love.

Love is the highest vibration on the scale of consciousness. It's what mystics are made of, it's what incredible leaders have. Love for themselves and love for life.

Here's where the white light meditation comes into play, let's say that's universal love. It's the consciousness that connects us to something bigger and better than we can imagine.

There are studies that have proven people healing out of the debilitating illness, injuries, depression, PTSD by following the method of white light.

Even if you are in the non-believer clan, just follow this meditation, let it flow in. Even if you don't understand, the white light is doing so much more.

Waking up every morning with a sense of purpose and clarity of mind is a habit that sets the tone for a fulfilling day ahead. To achieve this, I have found solace in a simple yet powerful meditation practice that helps me ground my thoughts and energy. This practice can be performed anytime and for however long you desire, but it's recommended to be done consistently for at least 21 days to see its full benefits.

This 21-day period helps establish the practice as an auto-replay in your subconscious, allowing you to connect to the light within seconds. The light is not just a metaphor, it's a representation of the infinite source of positive energy that surrounds us all.

The light is not just a metaphor, it's a representation of the infinite source of positive energy that surrounds us all.

We are all part of a collective, and the universe is all about vibrations that create our lives. Our thoughts, feelings, and actions in the present moment shape our future experiences, which is the basic principle of the law of attraction. By connecting to the light through this meditation, you are aligning your energy with the highest good, attracting positivity and abundance into your life.

The meditation is straightforward and requires only a comfortable place to sit with your feet on the ground. Begin by closing your eyes and focusing between your eyebrows, as if you are looking over a mountain peak in the distance. Imagine a beam of white light coming into your head from about 300 feet up. Feel or visualize the light filling your face, neck, throat, heart, stomach, legs, feet, and fingertips.

Imagine yourself surrounded by a column of light, like a shower, and feel the light grounding you to the reality of the fifth dimension. Allow the light to flow freely, and imagine any negative thoughts, feelings, or beliefs that no longer serve you being washed away with the light and going into the earth.

Some people are better at feeling the light, while others are better at visualizing it. Whatever works best for you, let the meditation be a personal experience and allow it to bring peace and calm to your mind, body, and soul. By making this a daily practice, you will find yourself becoming more and more connected to the light, experiencing its positive effects in every aspect of your life.

Just let the light in. The only way it does not work is if you say this does not work for me. As I mentioned, even if you are a non-believer, just go ahead and do this, you are about to be surprised.

Attraction = Inspired Action

The idea of manifestation and the law of attraction has always been intriguing to me, and I've spent a lot of time exploring and studying these concepts. While some may view them as a bit esoteric or out-of-reach, I've always found them to be highly practical and accessible. The key to manifestation is to understand that the laws are always present and available to us, but we must take inspired action in order to bring our desires into reality.

A great example of this is the story of a woman who wanted to get paid for sleeping. At first, this may seem like an impossible feat, but she decided to take inspired action and participated in a campaign with a mattress brand. To her surprise, she was actually paid to sleep 9 hours a day. The point here is that you can choose what makes you happy, and by taking steps towards your desires, they can become a reality.

When you choose something that you want to manifest in your life, the universe will start sending you signs and hints on what you need to do next in order to bring it into existence. However, it's important to remember that manifestation starts with a belief. You must believe that what you want is possible, and that it will come to you. Once you have that belief, all you need to do is follow the trail of small steps that will lead you towards your desires.

The Power Of Manifestation: A Guide To Bringing Your Dreams To Life

Have you ever found yourself longing for something more in life, but feeling unsure of how to make it happen? Or maybe you have a specific desire in mind, but it seems too far-fetched to ever become a reality? The truth is, you have the power to bring your dreams to life, and it all starts with the power of manifestation.

Manifestation is the process of bringing your desires into reality by focusing your thoughts and energy on them. It's about aligning yourself with the universe and letting the magic unfold. To get started with manifestation, the first step is to know exactly what you want. This may seem like a simple task, but many of us struggle to define our desires in a clear and concise way. We often talk about the things we wish would happen, but we don't take the time to really dive into what those things are.

This is why the first step in manifestation is so important. To begin, grab a piece of paper and make three columns. In the first column, write down your life vision. In the second column, write down your relationships. And in the third column, write down your contribution to the world. Take some time to reflect on each of these areas of your life and think about what you truly desire in each of them.

Biggest Part Of Attraction Is Clarity And Then Taking Action In That Direction.

First Action Is What You Want. How To Find That "Something"

Once you have a clear understanding of what you want, it's time to start visualizing. Visualization is a powerful tool in manifestation because it allows you to bring your desires to life in your mind. Close your eyes and imagine the exact car, color, and brand that you want. Allow yourself to experience the emotions of joy, happiness, love, and pride as you see others congratulating you on your new car.

Bring in all your senses and imagine the feel of the leather seats, the smell of the new car, and the rush of excitement in your heart.

After visualizing your desire, the next step is to show gratitude for it. Gratitude is a powerful force in manifestation because it signals to the universe that you are open and ready to receive what you want. So, take some time to express gratitude for your new car as if it's already a reality. This simple act of gratitude will help you align yourself with your desire and bring it closer to you.

The final step in manifestation is taking inspired action. This means taking small, deliberate steps towards your goal, trusting that the universe will guide you along the way. You may receive signs or hints along the way that will help you to see what steps you need to take next. Keep moving forward, trust in the process, and know that you have the power to make your dreams a reality.

This simple three-step process of defining your desires, visualizing them, and expressing gratitude is a powerful tool for manifestation.

By following these steps, you can bring your desires to life, no matter how big or small they may seem. And as you continue to manifest small things, you will build momentum and confidence, allowing you to bring bigger and more complex desires into your life.

STEP 01- Define The Vision

So, are you ready to start living the life of your dreams? Start with a clear vision of what you want, focus your thoughts and energy on it, and take inspired action towards making it a reality. Trust in the power of manifestation and watch as the universe conspires to bring your desires to life.

Take a paper, I love pen to paper, you can decide your own process. There is a hand and mind connection, which automatically opens up neural pathways that help you incept better into your subconscious.

Make 3 columns, in first column write life vision, in second column write relationships and third write contribution.

Column 1- Life View

The first column is all about how you want your life to look and feel. What is your vision for your body? How do you want to feel in your daily life? What do you want your career to look like? What kind of experiences do you want to have?

What is the vision for your experiences, where would you like to travel? How often, where and how do you like to travel. What house do you live in? What car do you drive?

Consider writing down at least 10 things you would love to have in your life, including health goals, experience goals, and career goals, with at least two items in each category.

For example, for your health goals, you may write down "regular exercise routine of 10 mins at least" and "healthy diet." For your experience goals, you may write down "traveling to new destinations" and "participating in new adventures."

Column 2- Relationships

The second column is all about your desired visions for relationships, including love, family, friends, and work. What do you want your love life to look like? What is your ideal relationship? Who do you want as your friends, and what kind of community do you want to have at work? Consider writing at least two items in each category, and feel free to write more if you feel inspired.

For example, in the love category, you may write down "finding a partner who supports and loves me unconditionally" and "having a strong and loving relationship with my partner." In the family category, you may write down "having a close and supportive relationship with my children" and "maintaining a positive and supportive relationship with my parents." In the friend category, you may write down "building a community of like-minded individuals" and "having close and supportive friendships." In the work category, you may write down "finding a job that I am passionate about" and "having a positive and supportive work environment."

You can write more but at least two to start with.

Column 3: Community

The third column is all about your purpose and contribution to the world. What gets you excited and what is your purpose for being here? This can be anything from being a great parent or homemaker to serving others in your community. Consider writing down at least five things that align with your purpose and get you excited about life.

What is the purpose that you are here for? Write what gets you excited when you think of doing, this doesn't have to be community service, it could simply even being a great parent, homemaker, anything, this could also mean that you would love to have an abundant life that would inspire everyone.

For example, you may write down "inspiring others to live a healthy and fulfilling life" and "making a positive impact on the environment." You may also write down "providing support and care for those in need" and "creating a safe and supportive community." Whatever your purpose is, make sure to write it down and hold onto it as a guiding force in your life.

When it comes to manifestation and bringing your desires into reality, it's important to start with a clear vision of what you want your life to look like. Writing down your goals and desires can be a powerful tool in helping you focus and bring your dreams to life.

By following this three-column process, you can get clear on what you want to manifest in your life and take inspired action to make it a reality. Trust in the process and know that with focus and determination, you can bring your desires to life.

Do this now, because you will either forget or "things" will come into the way and that "something" will not be uncovered. Go and finish this.

How did that feel? Getting the load off the brain and

just getting some clarity. It's beautiful. Now just pick up that list and highlight or mark the ones that get you excited. That really makes you feel, if this happens it'll be awesome. Yes those ones that bring a smile or butterflies in the stomach. If your list isn't exciting to you at the moment, spend some time, look for inspiration or do the light meditation and come back and rewrite it.

Once you have identified the aspects of your life that bring you joy and inspiration, it's time to solidify them in your mind. Start by reading them out loud, as if you are sharing your excitement with a close friend. After reading them out loud, repeat the process in a hushed tone, and then finally read them silently in your mind. This repetition helps to embed these desires deep into your subconscious mind.

Step 02 - Visualize:

Now that we have defined our visions, it's time to bring them to life.

Think of it as making a movie - we have the script ready, the characters in place, and now it's time to bring them to life. Don't worry about timing - it may take a few seconds or a few weeks, months, or years. Trust the process, do your work, and let the universe do its part. My goal is to teach you the basics so well that you can rewrite your own story the way you want it to be. This step is fun - it's about experiencing the reality you just wrote.

Every point you write will evoke an emotional response, and your body doesn't know if the feelings you experience are real or imagined. To fully embody your visions, you need to experience them with all your senses - bring in visuals, colors, feelings, smells, sounds, tastes, and touches. Close your eyes and visualize each point you wrote, adding as much detail as possible. If you want money, see your bank account with that amount. If you want a relationship, feel the emotions you would experience when with that person. If you want friendships, see yourself enjoying time with your friends, hear their laughter, see their smiles, feel their hugs. If you want a vacation, fully see yourself having the best time.

I've found that we often overestimate what we can accomplish in a year and underestimate what we can achieve in five years. I started this exercise and within a few months, many of the things I wrote down came to fruition. I wrote about visiting exotic places and having a supportive soul tribe, and all of it showed up within a few months. I didn't even realize how much had come true until I rewrote my goals a few months later. If you write 10 goals and 8 of them come true, isn't that better than not even writing down one?

Step 03 - Gratitude:

Our goals and movie are ready, and now it's time to add the lubrication - grace. Grace is the universe's benevolence that helps bring our visions to life. Our minds can't even comprehend how some things we want will come to fruition because we don't have all the data. That's where grace comes in - it's the guidance, the action steps, the gratitude, and the alignment.

Grace is like a filter that can brighten up even the darkest photos, bring out details, and make the movie magnificent. The third step is to express gratitude for what you just asked for. Don't thank the universe for something that hasn't happened yet, but express gratitude for the vision coming to life. Write or say "I am so grateful for..." and start with what you have. Be grateful for your body, for the vision, for the sunset, for food, etc. The feeling of gracefulness is just below the feeling of love - both are high vibrations that can help manifest your visions quickly.

Start small - make a list of five things you're grateful for and then read your 10 vision statements as "coming soon." The sequels are always more exciting because technology improves, and it's the same with life - be grateful for the life movie you're currently watching and look forward to the life movie sequel that's coming soon. Live in the feeling of "coming soon" - that something amazing is about to happen.

Remember, all growth requires action. You have to do the work for things to change, but there's no right or wrong way to do it. Try different things and see what you like best. Your approach will change and evolve as you do, so start where you are and watch your life change.

Shake Away

Have you ever observed athletes as they prepare to compete or boxers as they enter the ring? They give themselves a good shake from head to toe. This simple exercise is a natural response to getting into the present moment and into the body. The same can be seen in animals, as they periodically give themselves a full body shake. But why is shaking so important for our well-being and how does it help us stay in the moment?

Most of us live in our heads, often replaying past events or worrying about the future. We continue to dwell on the negative experiences that have happened and keep imagining what could go wrong. This is not unusual, as our minds were designed to look for danger so that we could survive. However, in modern times, this conditioning has gone into overdrive and our minds are constantly searching for potential harm. The problem with this is that it prevents us from moving forward and living in the present moment.

The past has already happened, and we must accept

it as an experience that has helped us grow. If we continue to dwell on it, it may be time to acknowledge how much our lives have improved since then. The future is uncertain and we cannot predict what will happen, so it is best to focus on creating a better present moment. We cannot change the past, but we can create a better future.

Shaking is a proven method to get out of our heads and into the present moment. Kids do it all the time, as they are naturally programmed to be in a state of joy and happiness. They bounce on their feet when they are excited and shake from head to toe when they are angry. This is the body's natural response to switch off the parasympathetic nervous system and get out of a low vibe. For those who are prone to overthinking, setting an alarm for every hour and taking a shake break can greatly benefit both the mind and body.

The act of shaking releases stagnant energy, helps muscles relax, and clears the mind. It is a simple and fun exercise that feels amazing for those who have sedentary or typing jobs.

To get started, stand with your feet slightly apart, shake your hands, and then loosen up your arms, shoulders, and legs. Add a gentle bounce to your feet by tapping your heels on the floor. Let all of your muscles relax, including your head, spine, and hips, and just enjoy the feeling. Breathe in through your nose and out through your mouth. Do this for three minutes, close your eyes, and feel the energy, the blood rushing, and the life flowing through you.

Stand with your feet slightly apart, shake your hands, and then loosen up your arms, shoulders, and legs. Add a gentle bounce to your feet by tapping your heels on the floor. Let all of your muscles relax, including your head, spine, and hips, and just enjoy the feeling. Breathe in through your nose and out through your mouth. Do this for three minutes, close your eyes, and feel the energy, the blood rushing, and the life flowing through you.

This exercise is also a part of the Qi Gong practice, where we channel energy to flow effortlessly in the body. Qi Gong is an ancient Chinese practice that involves moving the body in specific ways to channel energy and improve overall health. One of the simple exercises in Qi Gong is shaking, which helps practitioners release stagnant energy and improve the flow of life force (or "qi") in the body. This can lead to a feeling of refreshment, improved circulation, and a more relaxed mind.

Shaking is a simple and fun way to add life to the body and feel refreshed. Every muscle that has been carrying the weight of work is now open and fluid, allowing for a rejuvenating experience. Start your day with a shake ritual and shake off stagnant energy, embracing new beginnings and the beauty of life.

Shake out the old and stagnant and feel the renewal into ever cell.

You Get What You Give

The idea that we reap what we sow is a fundamental truth of life that has been recognized and celebrated throughout history. Our actions and the energy we put out into the world directly influence the experiences and outcomes we encounter. This principle is especially evident in our interactions with others. It's natural to be kind and considerate to the people we love and care about, but the real test of our character is how we treat others in our daily lives.

Being genuinely polite, offering compliments, and spreading positive energy can make a profound impact on the world around us. The people we interact with, whether it be the person serving us at a store or the cab driver transporting us to our destination, are all blessings in our lives. They play a role in making our lives easier and more comfortable, and it's important to acknowledge and appreciate their presence. The act of gratitude, no matter how small, can have a transformative effect on our relationships and interactions with others.

Moreover, how we treat others is often a reflection of

how we feel about ourselves. If we treat others with respect, kindness, and positivity, it can be a sign that we have a strong sense of self-worth and self-love. On the other hand, if we treat others with negativity and disrespect, it may indicate deeper insecurities or a lack of self- love. It's important to understand that our interactions with others are not just isolated incidents, but they shape and define our reality.

That's why it's crucial to start with small acts of kindness and positivity, no matter how small they may seem. Something as simple as smiling and saying "thank you" or silently blessing others in our thoughts can have a significant impact on our relationships and interactions with others. By taking these small steps, we can create ripples of change and make a difference in our own lives and the lives of those around us. Ultimately, the goal is to cultivate a life filled with love, kindness, and positivity, and to extend those values to others in everything we do.

Now blessings are kind of selfish, while you are blessing others you are inviting a better reality for yourself. So why not wish for others to be blessed so you can have more of what you want.

Have you ever had a moment where you felt like you just didn't connect with someone, despite your best efforts? I think it's safe to say that we've all been there. The problem is often rooted in pre- conceived notions that we form about people before getting to know them. We might see someone who seems uptight and assume that they won't be very friendly, or we might avoid someone because we think they're a snob. But these opinions are often based on limited information, and they can prevent us from forming meaningful connections with others.

Think about it, if we believe that someone is too uptight, we may be less likely to approach them and start a conversation. This is a missed opportunity for a potentially meaningful connection, as well as perpetuating a negative perception of someone who may be struggling with their own insecurities. The same goes for someone we believe is a snob. By avoiding them, we miss out on the chance to get to know them and potentially discover their positive qualities.

It's not just that these negative perceptions can be harmful to others, though. They can also be harmful to our own well-being and self-esteem. When we make judgments about others, we reduce them to a single characteristic or behavior, and this can prevent us from seeing the beauty and complexity of the human experience.

So, what can we do to overcome these biases and pre-conceived notions? Well, the first step is to challenge them. We need to be open to forming authentic connections with others and be willing to see people for who they really are, rather than just our perceptions of them. By doing this, we can expand our perspectives, build meaningful relationships, and cultivate a more positive and loving world.

Know there will be unpleasant people too, yes that's life, it's you don't have to take it personally, if there is so much drama in your own head, can you imagine how each one would have that too. Let's talk about how to deal with unpleasant people in a positive way! I mean, we all come across negative people from time to time, but that doesn't mean we have to join in on their drama. We can rise above it and spread positivity instead!

Here's what I like to do: I bless them. I don't mean just saying "bless you" when they sneeze, but I actually take a moment to silently send them well wishes. I might wish them good health, good fortune, or whatever else comes to mind. It's amazing how this simple act can shift my perspective and make me feel more positive.

And you know what? By doing this, we're also attracting more positive people into our lives. When we're on a path of growth and self-improvement, we naturally attract others who are also invested in their growth. So why not start now and make it a daily habit?

At first, you might think it's a lot of work, but trust me, it will become second nature before you know it. Just like learning to drive, play an instrument, or any new skill. Up-leveling your mindset takes effort at first, but once you get the hang of it, it's like you're on auto- pilot.

So, next time you come across someone who's a little on the negative side, try sending them some silent blessings. Watch how it changes your outlook and makes the world a better place. You won't be faking it, you are it.

The world is full of diverse individuals, and you will inevitably encounter them on a regular basis. Instead of engaging in negative behavior, try these fun and effective methods of interaction. When someone is shouting at you or being rude, simply gaze at them and ask in a calm tone if they are okay. The confusion in their expression often indicates that their outburst is the result of pent-up emotions that have not found an outlet. So, don't take their anger personally, as it's not directed at you, but instead a manifestation of their inner turmoil. Your simple query will change the trajectory of their thoughts, causing them to pause and reflect. This usually leads to a smile, as you have broken the cycle of their negativity.

If you suspect someone is lying to you, use your intuition and focus on their third eye, the center of their eyebrows. This will disorient them and put an end to the lie. If someone close to you is looking to argue, don't argue back, as the argument is not about being right, but breaking the cycle. Agree with them and the argument will likely fizzle out. People will be frustrated when they cannot start an argument with you, and they will eventually recognize their own aggressive behavior. You'll notice they will avoid future arguments with you, as they know it doesn't work for you.

When someone is yelling at you for no reason, make an effort to give them a hug if possible. If you can't, ask about their day with genuine interest. Yelling is often a way for people to vent their emotions that may stem from other sources, like work or other interactions. You can break the cycle by offering a compliment, showing empathy, or giving a hug.

If someone is being overly demanding or making unreasonable requests, take a moment of silence. They will often come to realize the absurdity of their request and will likely not bring it up again.

You stopped the chain.

When someone is yelling at you for no reason at all, make it a priority to go hug them if you can. In case you can't, then just ask them how their day was, be genuinely interested. Yelling is again just a way of venting out emotions that may be completely unrelated to you. It's a reaction to something that went wrong with them, be it at work, with other interactions. You broke the chain, just by giving them a compliment, showing empathy or giving them that hug. You broke the chain.

If someone is too demanding or makes an unreasonable request, stay silent long enough. Usually they would come to realize on their own how silly the request it and would probably not mention it again.

You broke the chain.

Always know hurt people, hurt people.

Always know hurt people, hurt people. Usually the unpleasant behavior of people has nothing to do with you at all, it is them having challenges that they are not ready for. If you were to lash out at them, you would just keep spreading the chain of hurt. Someone hurt them, they hurt you, you hurt someone you meet forward, and it'll be on and on. You can stop that chain at you by taking a different approach, because you are that powerful.

I call that a change reaction.

As simply as you can break the pattern of negative chain. You can start your own positive chain.

Once you decide to be the change, you can give that heartfelt complement, that gratitude, the blessing, out to someone which will help break their negative chain. When the same people go out on their day, your positive chain will help them be pleasant to whoever they meet. You became the catalyst for a beautiful change reaction and you don't even have an idea how many people that small action changed lives for.

Instead of following the pattern be the catalyst of change.

Everyday Ascension Codes

We've learnt so many methods to create a life that's extraordinary.

A life that's beyond what most people can imagine. The shifts and changes will show up immediately. I have seen my life change and I can vouch for everyone I've interacted with and how it changed their lives. My friends, my family, they are all part of the test subjects in some way or the other. Each of the code is very simple to imbibe in everyday life, it just needs your willingness. It's said that only 1% of people will take daily action, I'm hoping everyone who comes across this book will be either part of that 1 or be the change reaction and participate fully.

Ascension doesn't have to be an overnight success, you already know that's a myth. No success is overnight, it's the daily small steps that you take, each and every day that will shape reality. One day when you suddenly see that everything worked out much better than you expected. People who don't know your growth story will call it overnight success but you know it's the moment to moment choice, the work, the way you showed up is what you got here.

Life will keep hurling tower moments but these are the methods to parachute out of them. Look for mini expansions, reach out for the best good feeling thoughts. With this change, you'll experience rapid improvement in areas that previously took months of hard work to overcome. The transformation will allow you to quickly identify and overcome challenges, making progress faster and more efficient. The breakdowns are not happening to you, they are happening for you. Each and every experience is giving you a chance to become better and invincible. You are not just strong to get through, you are powerful to create your own story. You are the breaker of pattern chains and are the change reaction. The catalyst that will bring about a change in the world.

Remember to celebrate small wins because that's an invitation for the bigger ones to follow.

Rewrite your story as often as you want, rewrite your life goals as much as you want.

This is not about motivation, which disappears as

soon as the event is over, this is becoming, and this is the place where you shape shift into the most powerful version of you. You are the creator of your reality, you have the reins, you are the manifestor and you will thrive.

You no longer have to fake it to make it because you have become it. You are the ascended version, you are it.

Love and light.

Synopsis

Have you ever found yourself feeling stuck and unsure of how to level up in life? Are you tired of faking it until you make it and ready for a real transformation? This book is the guide you've been searching for.

Join me on a journey to define that "something" that's been holding you back, whether it be in your health, relationships, finances, or beyond. The concepts of manifestation, synchronicity, and purpose sound great, but why is it that not everyone is manifesting the life they desire? The answer lies in the subconscious mind and the program that's running on autopilot.

Through my own struggles and breakdowns, I discovered simple tools that have changed my life for the better. I have seen the shifts in myself and in others who have applied these methods. Trust the process, and be open to becoming, not just faking it.

This book is not just a collection of words on a page,

it's a personal testimony of my own journey to transformation. From hitting rock bottom and questioning everything I had worked for, to finding the courage and confidence to keep going. Let my journey inspire yours as we explore the ascension codes and learn how to truly become, not just fake it. It's time for Ascension.

Acknowledgements

My journey towards personal growth has been nothing short of extraordinary! I'm overflowing with gratitude for all the amazing people who have helped me along the way. I'm so thankful for coaches like Mindvalley, Ananda Sangha Delhi, Isha Centre, Christie Marie Sheldon and others, who have helped me uncover the hidden gems within myself and bring out the best version of me. Your guidance has been a beacon of light, illuminating the path towards a more fulfilling life.

I must also give a special shout-out to my amazing parents, who have always encouraged me to reach for the stars and never settle for anything less. You guys are my biggest source of inspiration and I'm so grateful to have you in my life.

And of course, I can't forget my readers and future fans! You guys are the reason why I do what I do and I'm so grateful for your support. Your belief in me gives me the courage to keep pushing forward and I promise to always bring my A-game.

Last but not least, a huge thank you to ChatGPT, my trusty editor, who has been by my side every step of the way.

So here's to all the amazing people who have helped me on my journey so far, and here's to an even more exciting future!

Let's make every moment count!

About the Author

Manisha is a dreamer who lights up the world with her spark. She is an enchanted traveler, having witnessed the most magnificent sunrises and the most exotic destinations. Her love for adventure and her thirst for life have led her to live each moment to the fullest. With every new day, she creates a reality more magical than the one before.

As a certified life coach and a visionary, Manisha is on a mission to inspire millions of people to break free from the limitations in their body, mind, and soul, and to unleash their limitless potential. She is a master of many trades, with hundreds of patented inventions, a yoga instructor, a motivational speaker, a bestselling author, and a storyteller like no other. Her expertise in animal flow, aerial yoga, Silva meditation, TFT, and mindset coaching has made her a renowned voice of inspiration and empowerment.

Manisha is a spiritual gangster and a breathwork expert, dedicated to spreading joy and creating a life that is nothing short of magnificent. Her teachings, drawn from her own personal experiences, emphasize the importance of self-love in unlocking one's full potential. A passionate advocate for self-empowerment, she is a shining example of the transformative power of love and a beacon of hope to all who seek a brighter future.

www.ingramcontent.com/pod-product-compliance
Lightning Source LLC
LaVergne TN
LVHW010635200726
843507LV00011B/1701